Frog Butts and Toad Warts?

Fascinating Frog Facts

AO PRESS

Written by Jessica Lee Anderson • Photos by Bob Ferguson II

Paperback ISBN: 978-1-964078-12-0

To Jesse Durham—frog lover and human extraordinaire. - JLA

To my kids Wes, Nate, Lily, Rebecca, and Zach for their inspiration and to my wife Julie, for her undying support. - BF

All photos taken by Bob Ferguson II apart from P. 32: Michael Anderson and Kat Barnhill

Names of species (current iNaturalist common names) clockwise from top left, unless otherwise noted: Front cover: Pine Barrens Treefrog; Copyright: Cope's Gray Treefrog; Dedication: Fowler's Toad on Eastern Box Turtle; P. 4: Red-spotted Toad, White-edged Treefrog, Blue-thighed Rainfrog (bottom); P. 5: Bahia Forest Frog, Yellow Cururu Toad, Eastern American Toad; P. 6: Coastal Snouted Tree Frog, Pickerel Frog, Mahogany Tree Frog; P. 7: Yellow Tree Frog, Masked Tree Frog, Palmar Tree Frog; P. 8: Porto Alegre Golden-eyed Tree Frog, Wood Frog, Eastern American Toads, Gray Treefrog; P. 9: Green-and-black Poison Dart Frog, Green Treefrog, Western Cottonmouth; P. 10: Yucatán Casque-headed Tree Frog, Fringed Leaf Frog, Crested Forest Toad; P. 11: Bischoff's Tree Frog, Pebas Stubfoot Toad, Marbled Tree Frog; P. 12: Common Reed Frog, Red-eyed Tree Frog, Ecuador Poison Frog; P. 13: Granular Poison Frog, Pale-striped Poison Frog, Green-and-black Poison Dart Frog; P. 14: Yucatán Rainfrog, Atlantic Forest Dwarf Frog (common name not in iNaturalist), Sharp-nosed Toad; P. 15: Gray Treefrog, P. 16: Emerald Glass Frog, Emerald Glass Frog, Fleischmann's Glass Frog; P. 17: Wood Frog, Eastern Spadefoot; P. 18: Fleischmann's Glass Frog, Fringed Leaf Frog, São Paulo Leaf Frog (common name not in iNaturalist); P. 19: Carpenter Frog, Northern Cricket Frog, American Bullfrog; P. 20: Couch's Spadefoot, Fowler's Toad, Couch's Spadefoot; P: 21: Cuban Treefrog, Pine Barrens Treefrog, Fowler's Toad; P. 22: Bocaina Tree Frog, Polka-dot Tree Frog, Mexican Burrowing Toad, Eastern Spadefoot; P. 23: White-lined Monkey Frog, Canelos Treefrog; P. 24: Southern Leopard Frog, Reticulated Poison Frog, Red-eyed Tree Frog; P. 25: Picos Tree Frog, Chocolatefoot Leaf Frog, Giant Monkey Frog; P. 26: Eastern American Toad, Spring Peeper, Pastures Rainfrog; P. 27: Fowler's Toad, Green Treefrog, Mexican Burrowing Toad; P. 28: Fleischmann's Glass Frog eggs, Eastern Spadefoot tadpoles, Wood Frog eggs; P. 29: Spotted-thighed Poison Frog, Pinocchio Rainfrog; P. 30: Giant Toad, Squirrel Treefrog, P. 31: Harlequin Treefrog, Chihuahuan Green Toad, Bahia Smooth-horned Frog; Back cover: Eastern Spadefoot

This Book Belongs to:

_____

Differences Between Frogs and Toads

Frogs and toads are amphibians, types of animals that can live in the water and on land.

Toads are a kind of frog that have the ability to live in drier places. Toads tend to have thicker skin—some even have bumps and lumps! Not all frogs are toads, and frogs can also have interesting bumps and lumps.

Toad Warts?

The bumps and lumps on toads may look like warts, but they are actually glands. Toads can't give you warts, though if they sense danger, they might squirt a toxic liquid from their glands that could irritate your skin. (They might also pee on you.)

Many toads and a few frogs have poison glands called parotoid glands that are located behind their eyes.

Super Skin

Like other kinds of animals, frogs shed their skin regularly throughout their lives.

Amphibians don't have scales and plates like reptiles. They can breathe and absorb water through their skin!

Are Frogs Slimy?

While many frogs live near sources of water, some species look extra wet because of a layer of mucus. Mucus keeps a frog's skin from drying out.

Besides keeping the skin moist and breathable, frog mucus contains protective chemicals.

Sensitive Systems

Frogs and toads are sensitive to changes in their environment. They're sometimes called "environmental indicators" as pollution or contamination is likely to impact them first in an ecosystem.

Chemicals along with fungi, bacteria, and more can pass through frog skin.

Predators or Prey?

Frogs are ambush predators. They sit in place waiting for a meal to walk or fly by them, usually whatever they can fit in their mouth. They don't chew—instead they swallow prey whole. Their eyes move into their mouth to push food down their throats. GULP!

Frogs are also prey for many kinds of animals. They are essential for a healthy ecosystem.

Fancy Features

Certain species sport spikes, spurs, crests, horns, and other oddities like flaps of skin. These fancy features may give an advantage in battle, finding a mate, or avoiding predators.

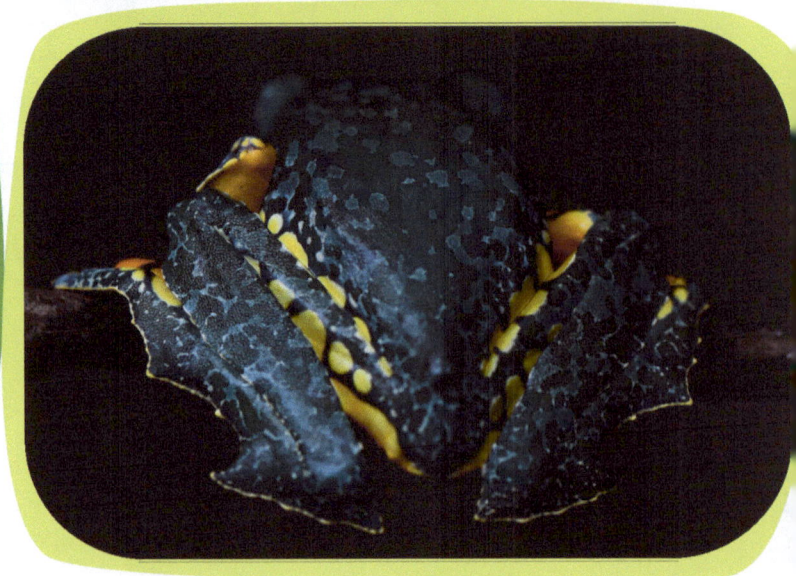

Patterns

Frogs and toads can have a variety of skin patterns like spots, stripes, and blotches. Patterns might also vary on a frog's backside, stomach, legs, hands, feet, and even toes. These patterns can confuse potential predators.

Kaleidoscope of Colors

Frogs with brightly colored eyes can surprise predators (this is called "startle coloration").

Some frogs showcase vivid colors and patterns to avoid predators and to attract mates. Even frog eyes can be colorful!

Poison!

Certain frog species absorb toxins from the things they eat. They store these toxic chemicals in their skin glands.

Aposematism is a fancy word that describes how predators learn to avoid prey with bright colors or patterns due to being dangerous or tasting gross.

13

Hide and Seek Champs

Instead of startling or intimidating potential predators, many frogs have camouflage adaptations that help them to survive. They blend into their environment.

Color Changing Frogs

Certain frogs can change colors depending on the time of day or a change in their environment. Others change colors as they age, from season to season, or during times of stress.

See Through Frogs

A few frog species are translucent like gummy bears—you can see through their skin and can even see their organs and bones! This makes it harder for predators to spy these frogs while they nap on the underside of leaves.

Extreme Survival Strategies

Frogs and toads in colder climates adapt to survive winter. Some hibernate in safe burrows near water that provides oxygen until spring. Select species can freeze over and thaw when temperatures warm.

In hot, dry climates, some frogs and toads will hunker down to conserve energy for a while (called estivation) until the rainy season starts.

17

Arboreal?

Frogs that live in the trees (arboreal) tend to have grippy toepads that help them cling to surfaces— even one-handed!

Aquatic?

Frogs that live in water (aquatic) usually have long, powerful legs. They sometimes have webbed toes that give them a swimming advantage.

Terrestrial?

Frogs that live on land (terrestrial) often have strong fingers for digging. Some even have claw-like toes or spades (sharp projections on their back feet).

Do Frogs Have Butts?

Frogs and toads have a cloaca—a tube that gets rid of waste. It is also part of the reproductive system.

Frogs and toads do not have butts built quite like humans. Frogs and toads don't sit on their rear ends in the same way people do either. That said, a few frogs look like they have human-like butt cheeks!

Excellent Eyes!

Many frogs have large eyes in comparison to the size of their bodies. Massive peepers let frogs spot predators in front, to the side, and even partially behind them. Frogs have a variety of pupil shapes (the black openings in the colored parts of the eyes).

Frogs that burrow or live in dark, watery environments tend to have smaller eyes in comparison to the size of their bodies.

Membranes?

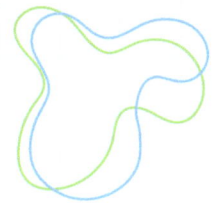

Frogs and toads have eyelids to protect their eyes, and they also have a nictitating membrane (sometimes called a "third eyelid"). Nictitating membranes shield a frog's eyes and keep them from drying out.

Most frogs have good hearing and have visible eardrums (tympanic membranes) near their eyes. (Not all species have visible eardrums.)

Do All Frogs Jump?

Many frogs are super jumpers! But not all frogs jump far or fast or at all—it depends on the species and the environment where they live.

Walking and Crawling

Jumping, hopping, and swimming are some ways that frogs and toads move. Others get around by walking or crawling.

Songs and Calls

Vocal frogs push air from their lungs past the voice box, through their vocal cords, and then back again.

Most frogs have the ability to create sounds, and they can sing without ever opening their mouths! Ribbit! Bark! Croak! Chirp! Scream! Each species makes a unique sound to find a mate.

Amplifiers

Some species have a vocal sac (or even two sacs) that fill with air to make their calls much louder.

Babies!

Most frog species lay jelly-like eggs that then hatch into babies called tadpoles. A number of species can lay thousands of eggs at once! These tadpoles then transform into adult frogs, a process known as metamorphosis.

Direct Development?

Some frogs will carry their babies on their back to protect them while they develop. A few frog species skip the tadpole stage entirely—they lay eggs that eventually develop into fully formed frogs. This process is known as direct development.

From Mini to Massive

There are over 7,000 species of frogs and toads in the world! Frogs and toads vary in size and weight depending on the species.

Fascinating Frogs

Frogs and toads can be found on every continent except Antarctica.

Scientists are continuing to discover species and learn more about these fascinating animals!

Jessica Lee Anderson is an award-winning author of over 75 books for young readers including the NAOMI NASH chapter book series. Jessica loves spending time in nature and exploring the outdoors with her husband, Michael, and their daughter, Ava! Jessica admires many Gulf Coast Toads near her home in Austin, Texas. You can learn more about Jessica by visiting www.jessicaleeanderson.com.

Bob is a naturalist with a compulsion to be outdoors. Wildlife conservation through entertainment, education, fundraising, and fieldwork is his mission and purpose in life. His organization, Fascinature, has donated six figures to saving land in the world's most biodiverse spaces. He even has a frog named after him! You can find him on Instagram @bob_ferguson_fascinature or sign up for his newsletter at fascinature.live.

Check out this book featuring more of Bob Ferguson II's photos:

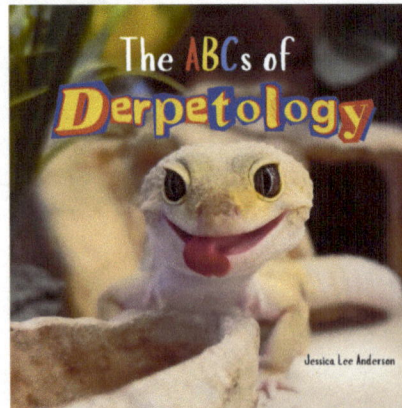

The ABCs of Derpetology

Jessica Lee Anderson

www.ingramcontent.com/pod-product-compliance
Lightning Source LLC
Chambersburg PA
CBHW061145030426
42335CB00002B/112